Here Comes the Sun

Dona Herweck Rice

The **sun** shines.

The sun gives
us light.

The sun keeps
us warm.

The sun helps
plants grow.

The sun gives
us **energy**.

The sun helps make
the **seasons**.

The sun helps us see
the moon.

We need the sun.

Let's Do Science!

How can the sun change water?
Try this!

What to Get

- ❏ 2 jars of water
- ❏ thermometer
- ❏ timer or clock

What to Do

1 Place one jar of water in a sunny spot. Place the other jar of water in a shady spot.

2 Wait two hours.

3 Put the thermometer in each jar. Have an adult help you. Which is warmer?

Glossary

energy—power

seasons—the four parts of the year

sun—the star that Earth rotates around

Index

Your Turn!

What do you need the sun
for? Tell a friend how the
sun helps you.

Consultants

Sally Creel, Ed.D.
Curriculum Consultant

Leann Iacuone, M.A.T., NBCT, ATC
Riverside Unified School District

Jill Tobin
California Teacher of the Year
Semi-Finalist
Burbank Unified School District

Publishing Credits

Conni Medina, M.A.Ed., *Managing Editor*
Lee Aucoin, *Creative Director*
Diana Kenney, M.A.Ed., NBCT, *Senior Editor*
Lynette Tanner, *Editor*
Lexa Hoang, *Designer*
Hillary Dunlap, *Photo Editor*
Rachelle Cracchiolo, M.S.Ed., *Publisher*

Image Credits: pp.5–6, 12–13 iStock; pp.18–19
(illustrations) Rusty Kinnunen; all other images
from Shutterstock.

Library of Congress Cataloging-in-Publication Data

Rice, Dona, author.
  Here comes the sun / Dona Herweck Rice.
    pages cm
  Summary: "It is time to learn about the sun."—
Provided by publisher.
  Audience: K to grade 3.
  Includes index.
  ISBN 978-1-4807-4529-2 (pbk.) —
  ISBN 978-1-4807-5138-5 (ebook)
  1. Sun—Juvenile literature. 2. Readers (Primary) I. Title.
  QB521.5.R53 2015
  523.7—dc23
                                        2014008928

Teacher Created Materials
5301 Oceanus Drive
Huntington Beach, CA 92649-1030
http://www.tcmpub.com
ISBN 978-1-4807-4529-2